15582

j743.6 Soloff-Levy,
SOL   Barbara.

How to draw farm
animals

JUL. 03 1993	DATE		
JAN. 01 1996			
NOV. 04 1996			
NOV. 06 1996			
DEC. 07 1996			
MAR 19 1997			
MAR 21 1998			
7-29-98			
AUG 2 6 2009			
AUG 0 9 2011			

© THE BAKER & TAYLOR CO.

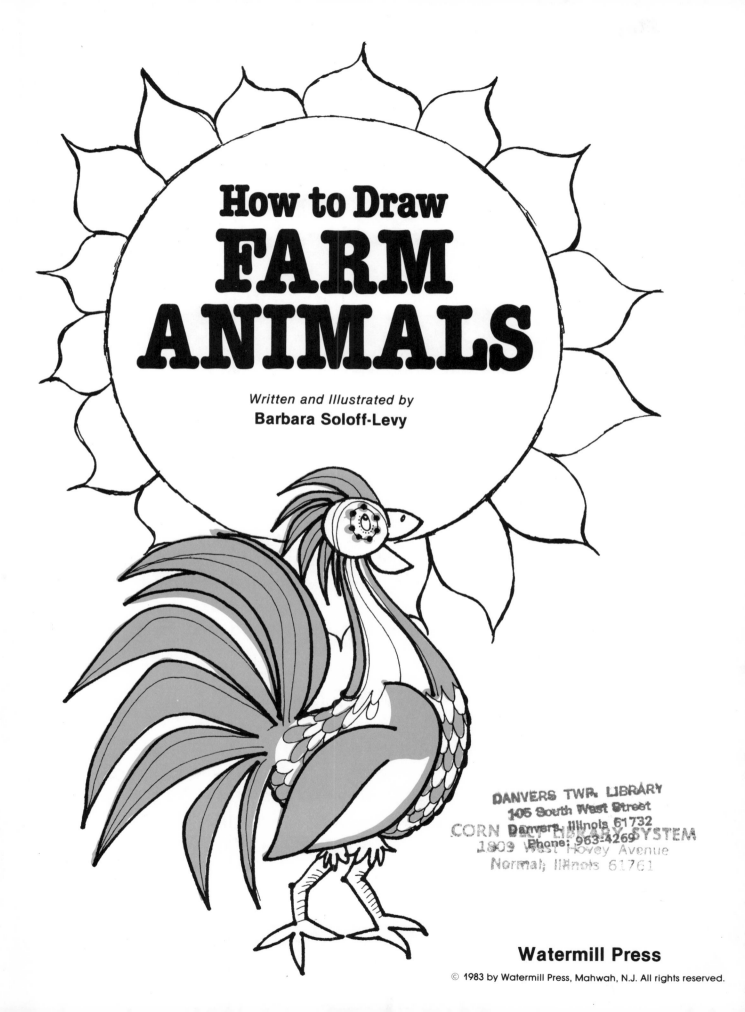

How to Draw
FARM
ANIMALS

Written and Illustrated by
Barbara Soloff-Levy

Watermill Press

Introduction

Farm animals are lots of fun to draw! Each of the drawings in this book is shown in several easy steps. Just follow each step, adding to your drawing as you go along. Soon you'll have a barnyard full of happy farm animals.

Before you begin your drawings, you might like to trace over some of the steps. This will give you an idea of how to draw the basic shapes used for each animal.

Start your drawing in pencil, so you can erase any unwanted lines. When your farm animal looks the way you want it to, go over your pencil drawing with a felt-tip pen. Next, color your animals with crayons or colored markers. Part of the fun of drawing is to use your imagination—so make your animals any color you want.

Each animal has its own characteristics. For example, a lamb has curly hair, a rooster has lots of colorful feathers, and a pig has a curly tail. While drawing, think of these features and exaggerate them. It will give your drawings their own special look. Most of all, don't be afraid to experiment. Now you're ready to begin—have fun!

Materials

(2) Number 2 Pencils
(2) Felt-Tip Pens
Eraser
Colored Markers or Crayons
Tracing Paper
Drawing Pad

CRAYONS

PENCIL

TRACING PAPER

PEN

DRAWING PAD

ERASER

Barn

Here are how the basic parts of a barn look. Put them all together, and you will soon have a fine home for your farm animals.

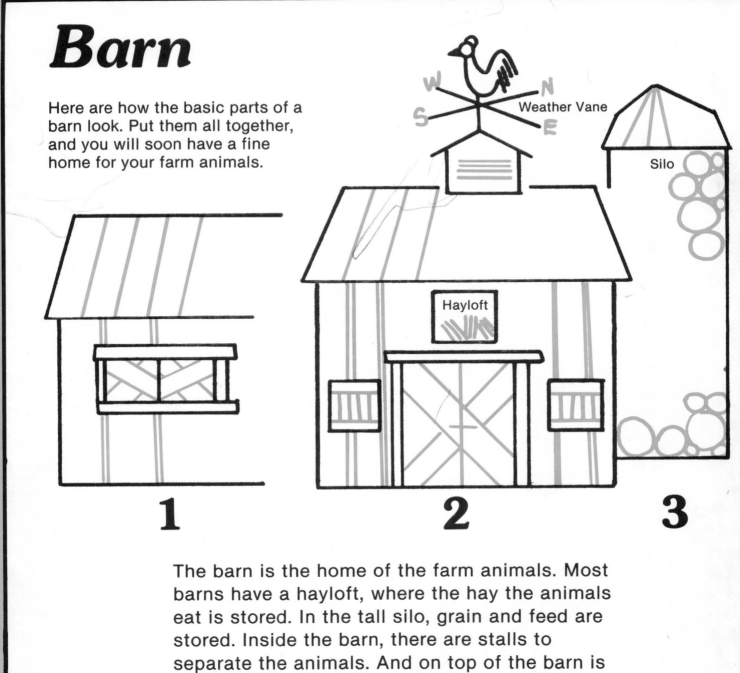

Weather Vane

Silo

Hayloft

1   2   3

The barn is the home of the farm animals. Most barns have a hayloft, where the hay the animals eat is stored. In the tall silo, grain and feed are stored. Inside the barn, there are stalls to separate the animals. And on top of the barn is the weather vane, which tells the farmer the direction of the wind.

Horses

Horses are some of the best-loved animals on the farm. They are fun to ride and are good friends to the farmer and his family. Often you will see the horses and their baby colts prancing in the fields.

Years ago, horses did much of the heavy work for the farmer. Today, most farms have machines to do this work, but the machines can't replace the devotion of a horse.

1

2

3

Sheep

Sheep often stay together in a herd, as they graze in the fields. During winter, a sheep's coat grows thick to protect it from the cold. In the early summer, the farmer cuts off the heavy coat of wool. This is called "shearing" the sheep. This wool can be made into yarn for clothes, blankets, and many other things. Baby sheep are called lambs.

1

2

1

2

3

Dogs

Every farm has at least one dog. This farm has Ollie, a very large Old English sheep dog. Ollie loves to herd the sheep so none run off. He also likes to romp and play with them. When you draw Ollie, notice how long and straight his hair is—it looks very different than the sheep's short, curly hair.

1

2

3

1

2

Cows

All day long, the cows and their baby calves graze in the pasture. Twice a day, the cows are milked, once early in the morning, and once again in the late afternoon. On a small farm, the cows are milked by hand by the farmer. Many large farms today have machines to do the milking. Cows are very important animals—the milk they give us is used to make cheese, ice cream, butter, and many other things.

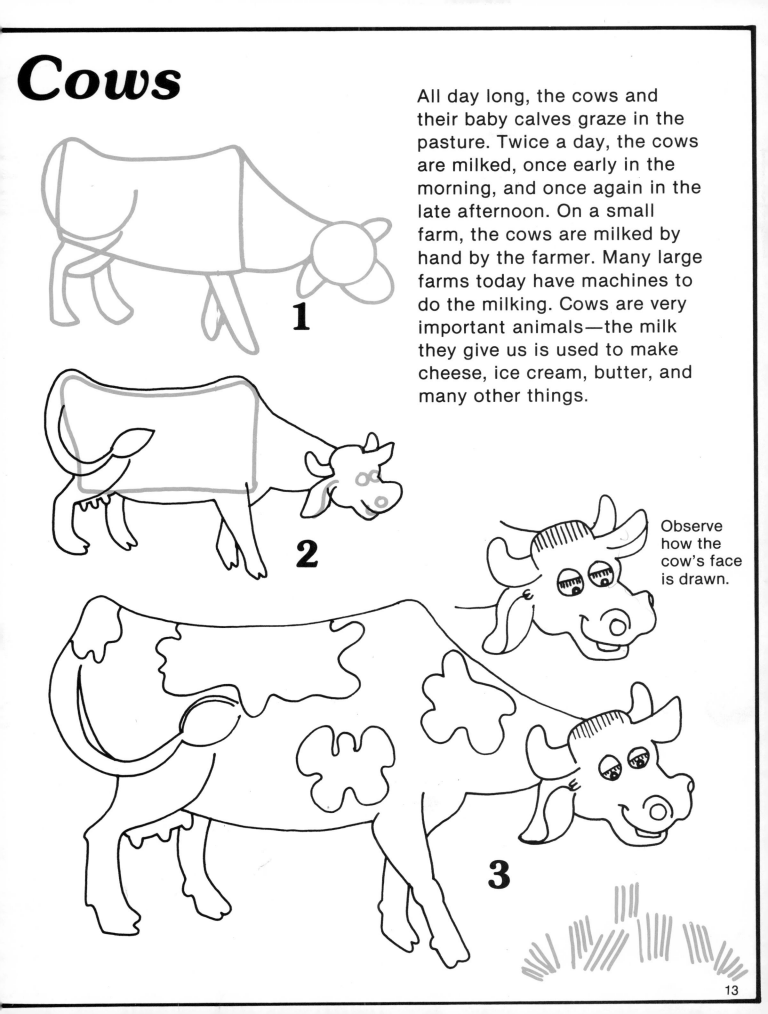

1

2

Observe how the cow's face is drawn.

3

Goats

What terrific lawn mowers goats are! They love to eat grass, leaves, bark, twigs, apples, and carrots. Goats and their babies, called kids, love to frolic, and they are extremely curious.

1

2

3

Goats have short, wavy hair. By drawing lines like these you can get this effect. Or, if you like, just color your goat.

Cats and Kittens

Look carefully at the basic shapes used to draw these cats and kittens. Practice drawing these shapes a few times to get the feeling of the poses. Then begin your picture.

1

2

1

2

3

Some cats have long hair. Others have short hair.

Cats have all kinds of markings.

"When the cat's away, the mice will play."

Have you ever heard this old saying? It's a very true one. Without cats, the farm would have too many mice. But cats work very hard to keep the mice away. The farmer and his family like to play with the cats and their soft, cuddly kittens.

Pigs and Piglets

Pigs are famous for rolling in the mud. But do you know why they do it? They cannot sweat—so to cool themselves they cover their bodies with mud. Looking at the tiny baby piglets, it's hard to believe some of them may grow up to weigh over 1,000 pounds (450 kilograms)!

Roosters

The rooster is known for waking everyone on the farm at the crack of dawn with his call—*Cock-a-doodle-doo!* A rooster is a male chicken. This spunky bird has a long tail and colorful feathers.

1

2

Decorate your rooster with all kinds of feathers.

3

The Sun

1

2

21

Hens and Chicks

Hens are female chickens. They like to eat grain and corn. They have beaks but no teeth, so to help them grind up their food, they also eat a bit of stone.

1

2

3

1

2

Draw these little chicks, too.

Hens lay many eggs, which take three weeks to hatch. Then out pops a chick—a yellow, feathery baby. The farmer collects the eggs that do not contain baby chicks. These eggs are used for food.

23

Turkeys

A male turkey is called a tom, and a female is called a hen. A fully-grown tom is quite large—he grows to almost 4 feet (1.2 meters) long. This bird is covered with beautiful feathers and has a very big tail. The hen is smaller and less colorful.

1

2

3

1

2

Feathers

Ducks and Ducklings

1

You're likely to find the ducks in their favorite place—the water. Nature gave them webbed feet to help them swim and fluffy feathers to keep them warm. Ducks may be many different colors, such as white, black, brown, blue, and green.

Water

A baby duck is a duckling. Have you ever seen a row of fuzzy, yellow ducklings swimming behind their mother?

2

Here's how the feet look when swimming. Note the webbed feet.

3

Farmers

Everyone on the farm has a job to do. Starting at sunrise, when the rooster crows, work begins. Taking care of the animals and crops keeps the whole family busy. Being a farmer is both fun and hard work!

Animals must be cleaned and fed.

1

2

1

2

Eggs must be gathered.

1

2

Seeds must be planted, and crops must be tended.

1

2

29

Farm Tools

Did you ever see a field of corn? It goes on for miles and miles. Did you ever wonder how all those seeds were planted and watered, and how each ear of corn was picked? Farmers have lots of tools and machines to help them. Here are some for you to draw.

Tractor and Seed Planter

1

2

3

Corn Picker

1

2

3

Fill the barnyard with your favorite animals!